Recycling Fun!

DECORATIONS, GAMES AND GIFTS TO MAKE

The Five Mile Press

Contents

1 Coloured Pencil Case

Experimenting with different textures of paper and cardboard will allow you to make fun and original arts and crafts. To make this pencil case, you can use any combination of colours. Or if you like, you can use a smooth piece of cardboard instead of ribbed cardboard and stick your favourite stickers on it.

You can choose any combination of bright and lively colours.

Tools and Materials

1 Cutting pad
2 Pencil
3 Ruler
4 Stanley knife
5 Scissors
6 Hole puncher
7 Glue
8 Metal paper fastener
9 Black piece of cardboard
10 Yellow ribbed cardboard
11 Coloured pencils

Coloured Pencil Case

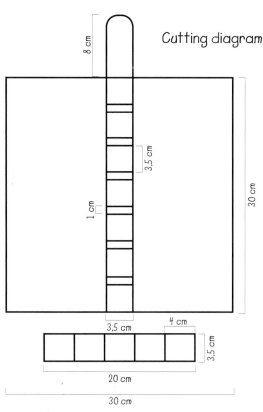

Cutting diagram

8 cm

3,5 cm

1 cm

30 cm

3,5 cm

4 cm

3,5 cm

20 cm

30 cm

1

First, cut a 30 by 30 cm square out of the black piece of cardboard. In the centre of one of the sides, leave a 3.5 cm wide strip of cardboard, which you will later use as a clasp to close the pencil case. When you have cut the square from the black piece of cardboard, mark two parallel lines in the centre of it that continue in the same direction as the clasp. These two lines must lie 3.5 cm apart from each other. Next, between these two lines mark twelve more lines that connect them. These lines must be cut two at a time. Mark the first line 3.5 cm from the edge of the cardboard, another line 1 cm from the edge, another line 3.5 cm from the edge and so on until the end.

2

Out of the yellow ribbed cardboard, cut some strips measuring 3.5 cm wide by about 15 or 20 cm long. You can cut the cardboard with scissors or ask an adult to help you cut it with a stanley knife. Next, cut these strips into smaller rectangles measuring 4 by 3.5 cm.

Ask an adult to help you cut these last lines using a stanley knife.

3

Take the rectangles of ribbed cardboard and insert them in the cuts that you made in the black piece of cardboard. The idea is that these pieces form a bridge on the black piece of cardboard through which you will insert the coloured pencils.

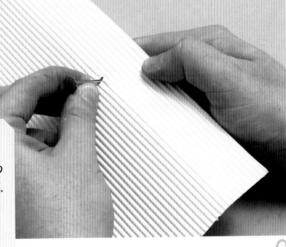

4

On the underneath of the black piece of cardboard, glue down the edges of the pieces of ribbed cardboard that you have just inserted. Press down so that they stick.

5

Using scissors or a stanley knife, cut a 32 by 32 cm square out of the yellow ribbed cardboard. Be careful when cutting because the ribbed cardboard can get ruined quickly. For this reason, you always have to cut on the smooth side of the cardboard.

To cut the ribbed cardboard it is better to cut it with a stanley knife. To be more efficient, you should mark all the material to be cut and then you ask an adult to help you. This way you will not have to ask for help every two or three steps.

6

About 3 cm from the edge, make a small cut in the centre of the ribbed cardboard. Insert the paper fastener in the cut, leaving the prongs of the fastener in the downward position.

Coloured Pencil Case

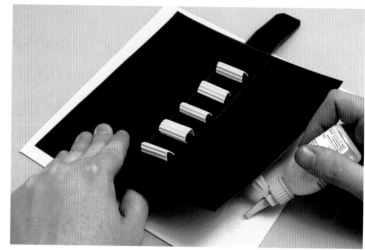

7

Glue the black piece of cardboard to the 32 by 32 cm square of yellow cardboard. Try not to make a mistake. You must glue on the smooth part of the ribbed cardboard and make sure that the tunnel-shaped strips of ribbed cardboard are facing upward.

8

With the hole puncher, punch a hole in the black piece of cardboard, which will act as a clasp, so that you can insert it into the head of the metal paper fastener.
In the pencil case, insert the coloured pencils in the tunnel-shaped strips of yellow ribbed cardboard which will hold them in place. Now you can close the pencil case by passing the paper fastener through the hole in the black strip. Your pencil case is complete!

2 Paper Spinning Tops

The spinning top is a fun toy that remains upright when you spin it due to centrifugal force. You can alter the effect by raising or lowering the circular cardboard on the shaft. It is also fun to observe the high-speed patterns that are produced when you spin the cardboard discs really fast!

Draw cool motifs on the spinning top.

Tools and Materials

1. Different coloured markers
2. Compass
3. White or coloured piece of cardboard
4. 6mm wooden shaft
5. Scissors
6. Pencil
7. Pencil sharpener
8. Stamping markers

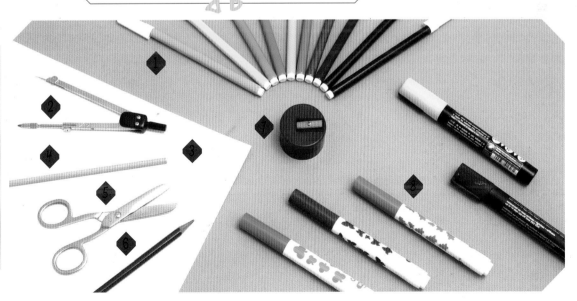

Paper Spinning Tops

With a compass, draw a 6 cm circumference. To do this, you must open the compass on a ruler and measure 3 cm, which will be the radius of the circumference. Make several circles before you cut them. This way, you will be able to make several spinning tops all at once.

Use scissors to cut the circle that you have just marked. You must cut each circle one at a time and do it very carefully, since it is important that the circle is quite precise.

3

You can use stamping markers to decorate in spirals, or make geometric shapes starting from the centre of the circumference. Your own imagination will dictate the spinning top designs. Stamping markers are markers that have a stamp on the tip instead of a normal drawing tip.

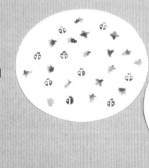

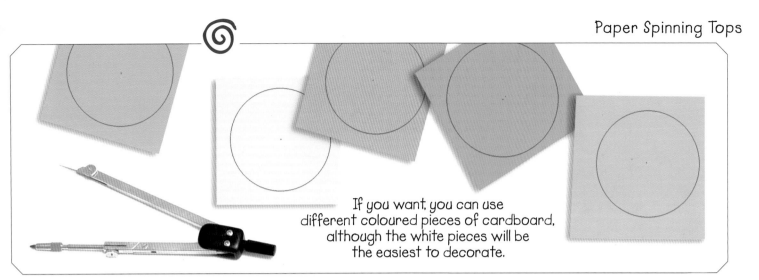

If you want, you can use
different coloured pieces of cardboard,
although the white pieces will be
the easiest to decorate.

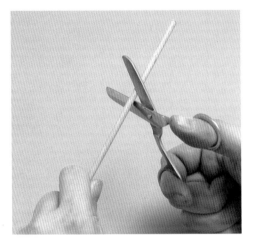

4

Use scissors to cut the wooden shafts
into pieces measuring 7 cm in length.
To make a more precise cut, begin by
marking the shaft with the scissors,
turning the shaft while you cut it.

If you intend to allow smaller
children to play with these
spinning tops, do not sharpen
the tip of the wooden shafts
too much because they
might get hurt.

5

With a pencil sharpener, sharpen
the pieces of wooden shafts that
you have cut as if you were
sharpening a pencil.

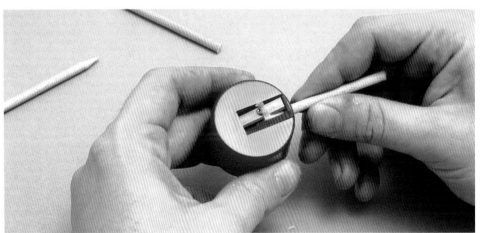

Paper Spinning Tops

6

Look for the centre of the circles, which will be the same hole that you have made with the compass. Use the sharpened tip to open the hole in the centre of the circles made from the piece of cardboard.

7

You can make as many spinning tops as you want, decorating them in many different ways. If you make spiral shapes starting from the centre of the circumference, you will obtain very fun optical effects when you spin the top.

3 Dominoes

Stamping with rubber stamps is a great decorating technique for crafts where the same image is repeated many times. This is why it's very useful to own a set of rubber stamps with different themes. If you want the rubber stamps to last for a long time, you should always keep them clean. So when you finish using them, don't forget to clean them thoroughly in water.

Tools and Materials

1 Glue
2 Cutting pad
3 Scissors
4 Stanley knife
5 Paintbrush
6 Ruler
7 Thick permanent marker
8 Pencil
9 Acrylic or tempera paint: red, blue and black
10 White piece of cardboard
11 Different rubber stamps
12 Cardboard

Dominoes

1

Cut three or four 30 by 6 cm strips of cardboard. You will get 10 domino pieces from each one of these strips if you do not make a mistake when stamping. To cut the cardboard, it is better to mark it with a pencil first. Then, ask an adult to help you cut it with a stanley knife.

Before you begin to stamp the piece of cardboard, test it on an old piece of cardboard to see how much paint you must use each time.

2

From the white piece of cardboard, cut another three or four 30 by 6 cm strips – the same measure as the cardboard. You can cut the piece of cardboard with scissors.

3

Once you have cut the strips from the piece of cardboard, you must mark the centre of them with a thick black marker. Then, using the same marker, mark 3 by 3 cm squares, as you can see in the picture.

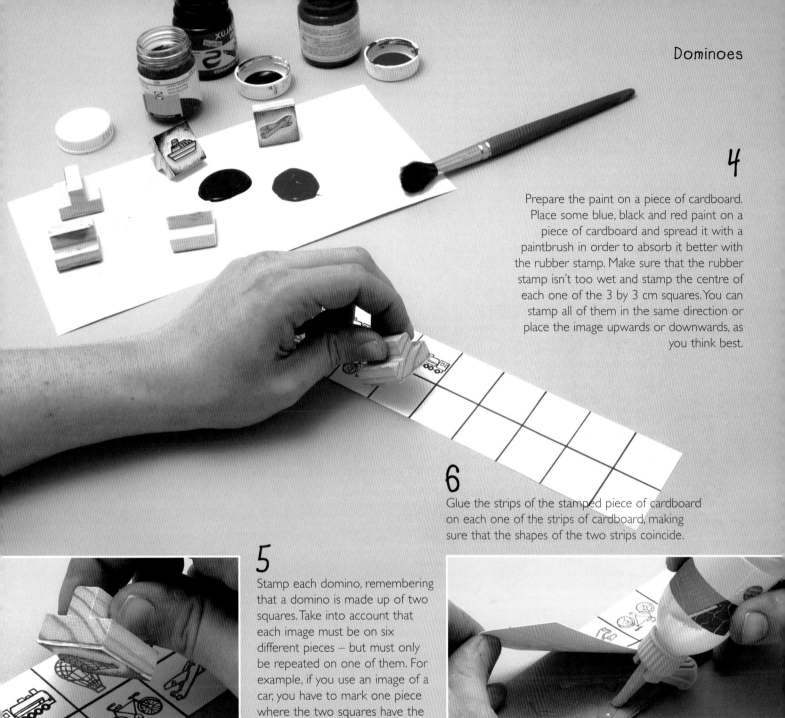

Dominoes

4

Prepare the paint on a piece of cardboard. Place some blue, black and red paint on a piece of cardboard and spread it with a paintbrush in order to absorb it better with the rubber stamp. Make sure that the rubber stamp isn't too wet and stamp the centre of each one of the 3 by 3 cm squares. You can stamp all of them in the same direction or place the image upwards or downwards, as you think best.

6

Glue the strips of the stamped piece of cardboard on each one of the strips of cardboard, making sure that the shapes of the two strips coincide.

5

Stamp each domino, remembering that a domino is made up of two squares. Take into account that each image must be on six different pieces – but must only be repeated on one of them. For example, if you use an image of a car, you have to mark one piece where the two squares have the same car and five other pieces with both the car stamp and a different theme.

Dominoes

Once the glue is dry, cut the cardboard dominoes through the centre of the short lines drawn with permanent marker. The dominos should measure 3 by 6 cm.

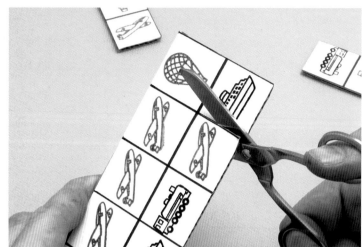

8

If you want, you can paint underneath the dominoes with black paint, as in the traditional dominoes, or with another colour of paint. Once you have cut out all of the dominoes, you are now ready to play with your own set of dominoes!

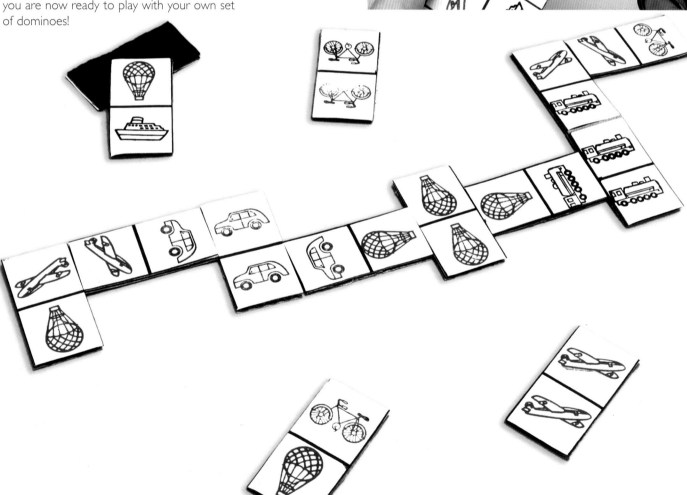

16

4 Cardboard Castle

To build this cardboard castle, you will need cardboard plus four cardboard tubes from rolls of aluminium foil or paper towels. For this reason, you should pay attention to the resources in your house when they run out, so you can use the containers to make fun crafts.

With little coloured pieces of paper and toothpicks, you can make fun flags to decorate the battlements of your castle!

Tools and Materials

1 Cardboard shoebox
2 Ruler
3 Pencil
4 Thick black marker
5 Cutter
6 Glue
7 White and black acrylic or tempera paint
8 Paintbrush
9 Red and white pieces of cardboard
10 String
11 Cardboard tubes

Cardboard Castle

1

On the cardboard tubes, mark the height of the sides of the cardboard box. With scissors, make two vertical cuts in each tube so they make a right angle. To make it easier, imagine that the hole in the cardboard tube is a watch and cut at the point that would be 12 o'clock and also at the point that would be 3 o'clock.

2

Take care that the opening is the right size so that it fits into the corners of the cardboard box. These cuts must match the length of the sides of the box. If necessary, you can cut another centimetre to ensure that the piece fits better, taking care not to damage the tube.

3

Fit the four cardboard tubes into the four corners of the shoebox. You must take care that all of the tubes are at the same height and that none of them become deformed.

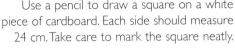

The box must be the same height on all sides, so the tubes that you can get should all be from the same type of product, whether it be aluminium foil or paper towels.

4

Use a pencil to draw a square on a white piece of cardboard. Each side should measure 24 cm. Take care to mark the square neatly.

5

Use scissors or a cutter to cut out the square that you have just drawn. If you prefer a straighter cut, ask an adult to help you cut the square with a cutter and a ruler, so you get a cleaner cut.

6

Put glue on one of the sides of the square. The glue must cover a strip that continues along the entire side of the square and cannot be wider than 5 mm.

7

With the square, form a tube, roll it up over itself and glue the opposite strip to the one that you have just put glue on. Press down for a while until the two sides of the square stick together.

Cardboard Castle

8

Next, on the shoebox, measure the length between the cardboard tubes. Transfer this measurement to the piece of cardboard and use it to form a rectangle that measures 6 cm by the measurement that you have just worked out.

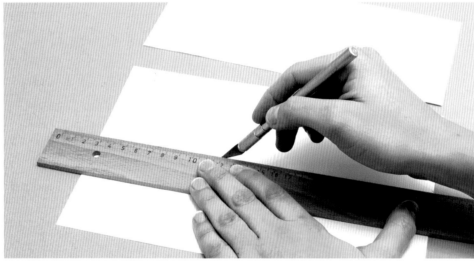

When you measure the length between the cardboard tubes, take into account that you will have two different measurements: one that is for the long sides and another for the short sides.

9

Cut out the four rectangles. To do this, you can use scissors or a stanley knife, although, if you use the latter, you will need the help of an adult.

10

Mark a line 2 cm from the edge of each one of the rectangles that you have just cut out.

11

Once you have drawn this line, make some marks on it every 2 cm. Trace a straight line between these marks and the side of the rectangle.

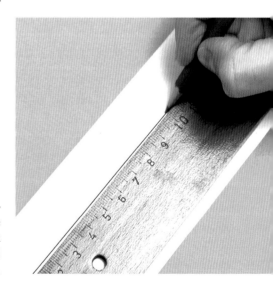

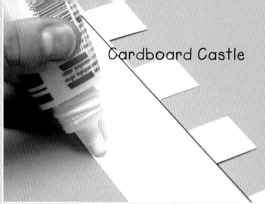

12

Use scissors to cut the small marks that you have just made.

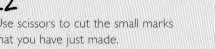

If you see that you have gone over the measurement, you can cut away what is left over on the boxes.

13

Cut out every second space. This way you will form the typical shape of castle battlements.

14

Measure the perimeter of the cardboard rolls, and then the perimeter of the rolled-up piece of cardboard that you made earlier with the 24 cm square. From the piece of cardboard, cut rectangles with the dimensions of 6 cm by the measurements that you have just made, the same as you did with the sides of the box. Repeat the same process of marking and cutting 2 cm into the pieces of cardboard to form the battlements, and then cut them out.

15

Glue on the pieces of cardboard for the sides of the box and for the tubes in the corners of the box.

Cardboard Castle

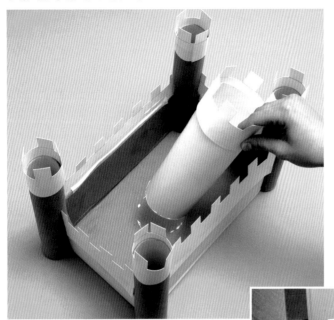

16

Once you have glued on all the pieces of cardboard used for the castle's battlements, put a little glue in the centre of the box and on the bottom part of the tube that you have just made out of the 24 cm square piece of cardboard.

For the castle base, you can decorate a piece of cardboard with the motifs that you like the most: a moat, flowers, animals, etc...

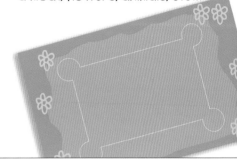

17

With a pencil, draw a door in the centre of one of the short sides of the castle. Take care that the door is centred on this side of the cardboard box.

18

Use a cutter to cut out the door that you have just drawn. It is a somewhat complicated process because you have to pierce the cardboard with the cutter first and then cut firmly, so you will have to ask an adult to help you. Cut out the shape of the door except for the side touching the ground.

19

Use the cutter to make four holes in the upper part of the door. Two of them must be made on the cardboard of the door itself and the other two must be made on the cardboard of the castle wall, as shown in the picture. Pass two pieces of string through these holes and tie a knot at the ends, so that the strings do not slip through the holes.

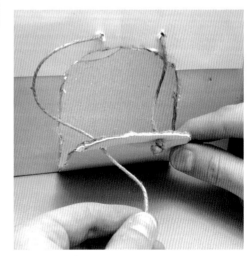

You can make some trees by sticking a toothpick in green foam and gluing on some treetops that you have drawn and cut out.

20

In a jar or on a plate, prepare some white acrylic or tempera paint and add some black acrylic or tempera paint to create a grey colour. Mix the paints with a paintbrush. You must mix them well so that the grey colour is smooth.

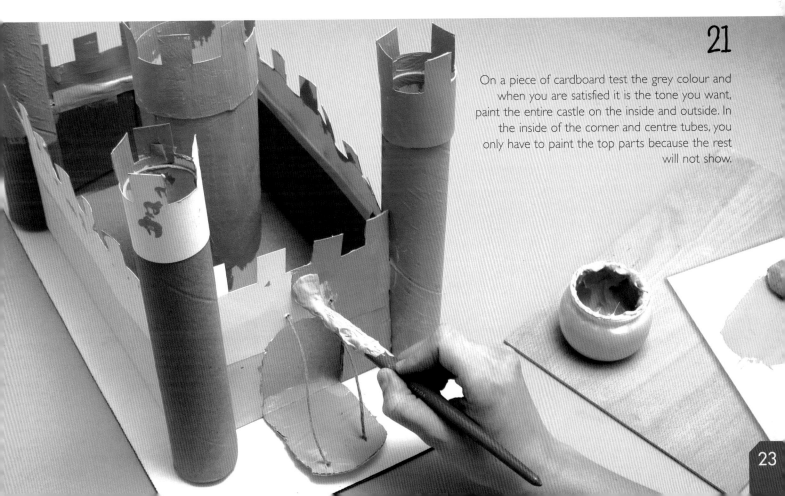

21

On a piece of cardboard test the grey colour and when you are satisfied it is the tone you want, paint the entire castle on the inside and outside. In the inside of the corner and centre tubes, you only have to paint the top parts because the rest will not show.

Cardboard Castle

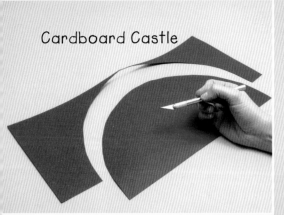
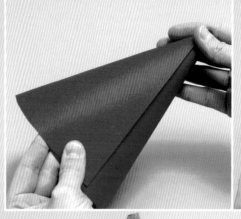

22

Draw a semicircle on a red piece of cardboard, which should be a half-circle with a diameter measuring approximately 24 cm. Use scissors or a stanley knife to cut it out.

23

Fold the red piece of cardboard over itself, as shown in the picture. Place glue on the sides of the cone and press them down for a couple of minutes until they completely stick together.

24

Put the cone in its place on the tower, and if you want, paint bricks or uneven stones on the outside of the castle. Now you can put your castle on display or even play toy soldiers in it!

5 Animal Mobile

Mobiles are fun decorations to make and will look great in your room once you hang them from the ceiling! Because of its light structure, any puff of wind will cause the mobile to spin and move around, even when no one is in the room. To make this mobile, we will use colourful cardboard animals.

You can use any animals or figures that you like. You can even make cardboard aeroplanes that will look like they are flying!

Tools and Materials

1. Cardboard
2. Cutter
3. Scissors
4. Several different colours of acrylic or tempera paint
5. A 65 centimetre long wooden shaft
6. Pencil
7. Black permanent marker
8. Paintbrush
9. Fishing line
10. Glue

Animal Mobile

1

Use a pencil to draw four animals on a piece of cardboard. It is important that you draw the front of the four animals first and mark all of the details well with a pencil.

If you want, you can outline the details of the animal figure with a thick black marker. This way, you will make your animal look more alive and dynamic, accentuating their fiercer or nicer features.

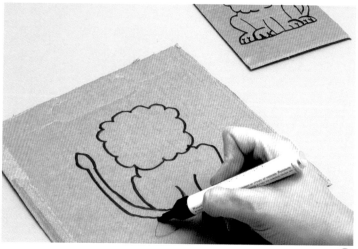

2

When you have drawn the front of the four animals, draw the back of them on another piece of cardboard. To do this, you can cut out the front of the same animal figure and trace it on the new piece of cardboard.

3

Paint the different animal drawings with acrylic or tempera paint, using the colours of your choice. If you want a realistic mobile, use each animal's real colours, although if you want, you can be more original by painting the animals with more original colour combinations.

4

Paint the back of the animals using the same tonal range that you have used for the front part of each of them.

5

Since the mobile will move constantly and both sides of the animal will be seen, it is important that you are careful about the details, taking into account that the characteristics on the back and front must correspond with each other.

6

Cut out both sides of the animal figures. Take care that the cuts are precise, since both parts of each animal must fit together.

When you cut out the details of the cardboard animals, it will be better if an adult helps you use the cutter. This way, you will be able to cut between the cardboard in the smaller spaces.

7

Paste the unpainted part of each half of the animal with white adhesive or glue. Take care to spread the glue or adhesive and let it dry a few seconds before you stick the two halves of the animal together.

Animal Mobile

8 To see if the glue has dried enough, you must test it by sticking the two halves of the cardboard animal together and then separating them. If little threads of glue form between the two halves, this means that you can now firmly stick them together; otherwise, you should wait a little longer.

9

Once the glue has dried for a few moments, stick the two halves of each animal together, taking care not to make a mistake and glue the wrong side!

10

Press the two halves of each animal down for a couple of minutes, so they stick together better. You will want to have the two halves neatly glued and firmly stuck together, because any defects will show when the mobile moves.

Pre-plan where you will make the hole for the string to pass through. This way you will make sure that the animal hangs in the correct position.

11

Use the point of the scissors or the tip of the stanley knife to make a hole in the upper and middle part of each animal. The fishing line will pass through these holes.

12

Take the wooden shaft and, using the ruler, measure two segments or pieces; one of 30 cm and another of 35 cm. Use a pencil to draw a mark around the shaft.

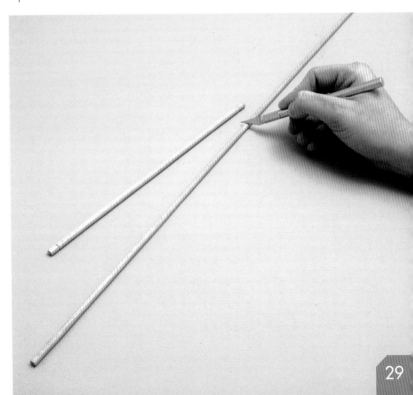

13

With the cutter or scissors, cut the wooden shaft where you have just made the marks. Ask an adult to help you cut the wooden shaft.

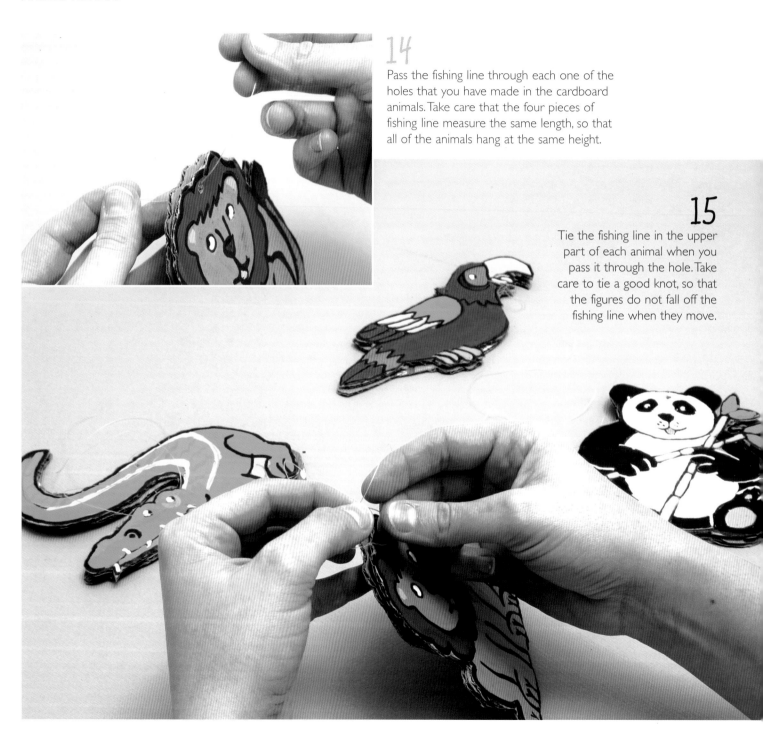

14

Pass the fishing line through each one of the holes that you have made in the cardboard animals. Take care that the four pieces of fishing line measure the same length, so that all of the animals hang at the same height.

15

Tie the fishing line in the upper part of each animal when you pass it through the hole. Take care to tie a good knot, so that the figures do not fall off the fishing line when they move.

30

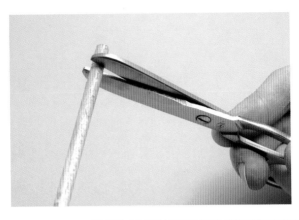

16

With the scissors, carve a groove 1 cm from the ends of each piece of shaft that you have cut. This way, you will make sure that the fishing line does not slide on the wood.

To carve the grooves, you must press the scissors down a little on the wood, as if you were going to cut it, and, then, while you continue to press down, rotate the wood.

17

Using the fishing line, tie one of the animals on each end of the pieces of the wooden shaft. Take care that all of the pieces are tied at the same distance from the wooden shaft, so that the weight is balanced.

18

Criss-cross the two wooden shafts, attaching them to each other with more fishing line. If you want to secure the joint, you can use a drop of glue or else carve a groove with the scissors in the middle part, so that the fishing line does not slide.

Animal Mobile

19

Now you can hang the mobile from the ceiling of your room. If you see that one side is not balanced because some of the animals weigh too much, you can correct this by rolling up and shortening the fishing line on the wooden shaft of the animal that is opposite to the animal that is hanging too high.

6 Desk Set

In this activity you will learn how to use folded and covered cardboard to make three-dimensional pieces, such as tailor-made boxes or trays for you to store things in. Here you will learn how to make a decorated desk set, which can be a good gift idea for your friends.

Tools and Materials

1. Wrapping paper
2. Eraser
3. Ruler
4. Coloured pencils
5. Pencil
6. Compass
7. Scissors
8. Stanley knife
9. Cardboard
10. Cutting pad
11. Thick cardboard tube about 10 cm high by 5 cm wide
12. Thick glue stick

Desk Set

1

Take a sheet of cardboard and mark a 22 by 17 cm rectangle on it. Mark a parallel line on each side of the rectangle 3 cm from the edge of the cardboard, like you see in the pattern. Copy the pattern by drawing four 3 cm squares and the lines joining them. Mark the latter lines with discontinued pencil strokes so that you know later where you will have to fold along, as opposed to where you will cut.

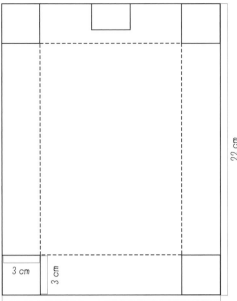

Cutting diagrams

22 cm

3 cm

3 cm

17 cm

3 cm

8 cm

17 cm

2

Mark a 3 by 2 cm rectangle on one of the two short sides. Remember how it is marked on the pattern, since later you will have to cut it out.

3

Once you have marked the cutting and folding lines, the rectangle that you have drawn should look like the one that appears in this picture.

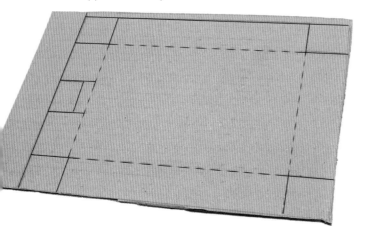

4

Take another piece of cardboard and mark a 17 by 8 cm rectangle on it.

5

At the edges of the rectangle, mark three parallel lines that are 3 cm away from the sides. These lines must continue along the two short sides, that is to say, the 8 cm sides and one of the 17 cm long sides. If you look at the second pattern, you will see that two 3 cm squares appear in two corners. Mark broken lines that emerge from these squares, as is shown in the pattern.

Whenever you have to draw a circle, you must open the compass as wide as the radius of the circumference which is half of the diameter.

Desk Set

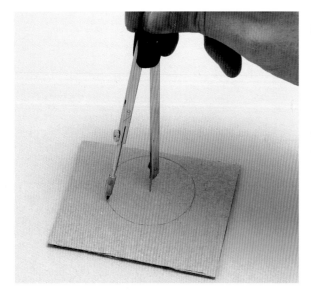

6 On a smaller piece of cardboard draw a circle with a 5 cm diameter. To do this, you have to open the compass 2.5 cm, which will be the radius of the circumference that you draw.

In a pattern, the broken lines indicate the place where you must fold and the solid lines indicate where you must cut.

7 Use scissors or a stanley knife to cut out the cardboard rectangles that you drew earlier. If you prefer to use a stanley knife so that the cut is cleaner, ask an adult for help. For now, you must only cut along the exterior lines of the rectangle.

8 Next, using scissors or the stanley knife, you can cut out the squares in the corners. Be careful not to cut any broken lines because these lines indicate where you must fold.

9

Cut the small rectangle just as you have done with the first one. It is important that the cuts are very straight, so ask an adult for help.

10

Next you must cut out the squares in the two corners of the small rectangle, as well as the cardboard circle that you drew earlier. Now you will have the three basic elements for your desk set.

11

On the underneath of the wrapping paper, mark three rectangles: two measuring 20 by 12 cm and the other measuring 25 by 22.5 cm.

Desk Set

12

Cut the two traced drawings out of the wrapping paper. To cut this type of paper you must always use scissors, since the stanley knife can affect the paper fibres and ruin the paper.

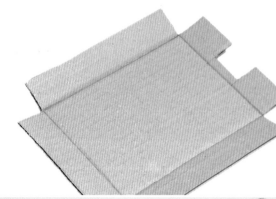

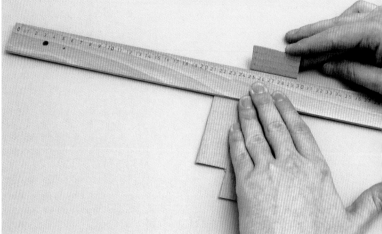

13

Fold along the broken lines that you have marked on the cardboard rectangles. A good technique for making a straight fold along the line is to place a ruler on the broken line and fold the cardboard against the ruler, as shown in the picture.

14

Take the rectangle that you have cut out of wrapping paper for the cardboard tube, that is to say, one of the 20 by 12 cm rectangles, and make some cuts in the two long sides of the paper. The cuts must be very small – 1 cm at the most.

15

Use the glue stick to spread glue over the entire back of the piece of wrapping paper that you have just cut out. You must cover it completely and take care that there aren't any lumps of glue on the paper.

16

Place the tube in the centre of the wrapping paper and, starting from one of the short ends, roll it up with the paper until it is totally covered.

17

Insert the leftover paper in the two holes of the tube. You will see that when you have made the cuts on the sides of the paper, it will be easier for you to fold in.

18

When you have finished covering the tube with paper, paste the cardboard circle on the wrapping paper that you prepared earlier. You must paste glue on the entire paper circle before pasting the cardboard circle on top of it.

Desk Set

19

Paste the cardboard circle on one of the ends of the covered tube. If you have measured correctly, the cardboard circle will fit over the tube's hole. Don't forget to paste glue on the uncovered part of the circle as well, so that it sticks to the tube.

20

Take the 25 by 22.5 cm wrapping paper rectangle, and use the glue stick to cover it completely.

Although a glue stick is cleaner than liquid glue, you must always take care that there are not any lumps or pieces of thin cardboard or paper stuck in the place where you are going to use it, since, otherwise, it will show and cause the delicate paper to wrinkle.

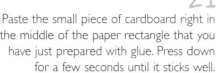

21

Paste the small piece of cardboard right in the middle of the paper rectangle that you have just prepared with glue. Press down for a few seconds until it sticks well.

22

Paste a little glue on the three flaps of the piece of cardboard. The flaps are the pieces of cardboard that you will later have to fold upwards.

23

Fold the wrapping paper over the flaps of the shortest sides of the cardboard, as you see in the picture. Take care that they stick firmly before you continue.

24

Fold the bottom part of the paper and paste it directly on the piece of cardboard that you are not going to fold. It is advisable that the wrapping paper is straight because otherwise the drawing on the paper will look slanted once you assemble the tray.

Desk Set

25

Now fold and paste down the last side of the wrapping paper for the flap, which you will fold along the longer side. Once you have done this, you will have a decorated paper rectangle.

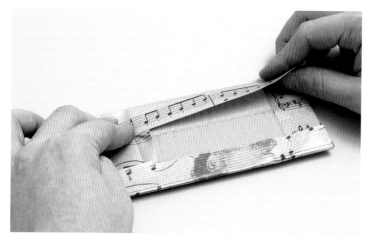

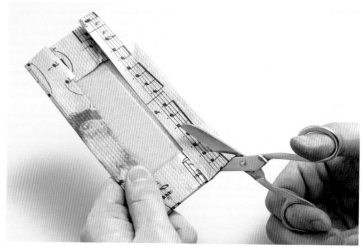

26

On the two corners of this rectangle where there is not any cardboard, cut the wrapping paper starting at the outside corner and right up until the point where there is cardboard again, as you see in the picture.

27

Once you have made the cut, you will have two pieces of paper, one at each side, that are not glued. These pieces of paper will help you to join the flaps that you are going to fold. Paste glue on these strips of paper and fold the strips of cardboard along the marked spot.

28

Once you have folded the strips of cardboard, you can paste the strips of paper that you have just covered with glue. This way it will look like the shape that appears in the picture. Repeat the same operation on the other side.

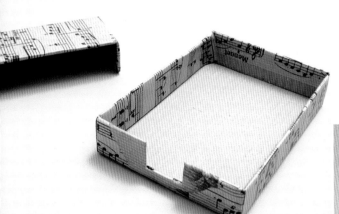

29

Using the same technique, you must cover the other bigger piece of cardboard. You can do it the same way as you just did, and when you reach the middle point, cut the paper and fold it towards the inside of the cardboard tray until you obtain a shape like the one shown in the picture.

30

Fit one of the two pieces of rectangular cardboard inside the other, and you will have your own desk set to keep your pencils and notes in. As you can see, it doesn't matter what wrapping paper you use, but remember that whatever you choose, it must be thick so that the glue does not show.

1 Jigsaw Puzzle

The jigsaw puzzle is a very fun game that you can create with your favourite pictures, and when you get tired of playing with it you can leave it assembled as a picture of your favourite cartoon or movie character. You can change the picture just by turning the pieces. You surely cannot do this with a normal puzzle!

You can choose any picture you like, or even a drawing that you have drawn and coloured yourself!

Tools and Materials

1. Thin white cardboard
2. Stanley knife
3. Scissors
4. Cutting pad
5. Ruler
6. Adhesive tape
7. Pencil
8. Marker
9. Sheets of paper with illustrations of your favourite characters
10. Embossing tools
11. Glue stick

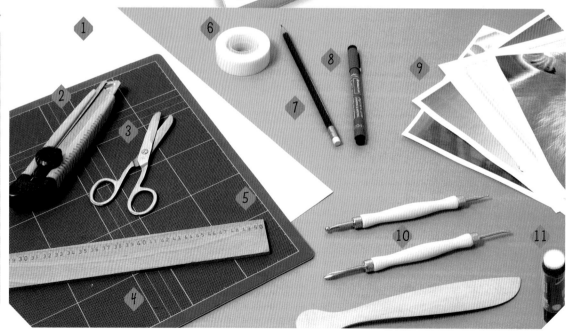

1

Draw a 29 cm (**a**) by 21 cm (**b**) rectangle on a thin white piece of cardboard. Use one of the corners of the thin cardboard to make this rectangle, so that you only have to cut two of the four sides.

2

Next, on the 29 cm vertical line, draw two parallel lines at a distance of 6 cm (**c**) from the edges of the rectangle.

3

Across the lines that you have just drawn, draw some more lines at a distance of 8 cm (**d**) from the upper edge of the rectangle and another line, parallel to this line, at a distance of 15 cm from the upper edge (**e**), or what amounts to the same thing, at a distance of 7 cm from previous line (**f**).

4

Parallel to the 29 cm lines that you have marked at a distance of 6 cm, draw two more broken lines at a distance of 7 cm from the edge (**g**). Draw another horizontal line 7 cm long from the bottom edge (**h**). Also draw diagonal lines that connect the 29 cm parallel lines at the intersection with the horizontal lines.

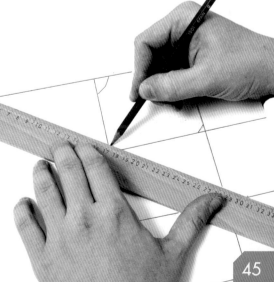

Cutting diagram

b

1 cm

8 cm d

6 cm

c

a

7 cm f

e 15 cm

7 cm h

d 8 cm

6 cm

c

e 15 cm

f 7 cm

7 cm h

7 cm h

7 cm

g

7 cm

g

1 cm   1 cm

21 cm

Jigsaw Puzzle

Cut out the shape that you have just drawn.
It should be a figure in the shape of a cross.

Now, cut out the small triangles that have been formed at
the intersections of the horizontal and vertical lines.

7

Once you have the
measurements of the
pattern and you have
correctly cut the shape out,
trace the shape eleven
times on the white thin
cardboard. You should have
twelve equal shapes.

8

Use scissors to cut out all of these shapes. You must be very careful with the measurements because the pieces of the jigsaw puzzle must all be the same size.

9

Use the embossing tool to flatten the folding lines of the pieces that you have just cut out. Use the embosser like a pencil, marking the folding lines using a ruler.

10

Once you have done this, fold the thin cardboard along the marks with the assistance of a ruler, which will help you to obtain a more perfect fold. Begin folding the flaps of the longitudinal part of the piece, as shown in the picture.

11

Using the ruler, fold the lateral squares of the cross, just as you have folded the previous flaps.

Jigsaw Puzzle

12

Now, fold down the top of the squares as you can see in the picture.

13

With a glue stick, paste all of the flaps of the cross. Be careful not to go over the folding lines.

Embossing tools are tools that are normally used to work on tin or engravings. They are easy to find in any craft store.

14

Take the cardboard by its longitudinal side and, folding along the line, connect the top flap with the bottom part of the fold.

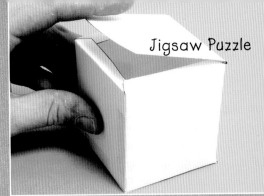

15

To obtain a stronger box, you can use a little adhesive tape to reinforce the glued flaps and make the shape of the box more secure.

16

Stick the adhesive tape on well and make sure that the box or cube shape is completely closed and that you have not gone over the folding lines.

17

Fold the lateral squares and stick them to the flaps of the cube-shaped box that you have just assembled. If necessary, you can paste more glue on the thin cardboard.

18

Repeat this process with the other eleven pieces that you have cut out, so that you obtain twelve more identical cubes.

Jigsaw Puzzle

19

Get ready to begin gluing the illustrations on the cubes of the jigsaw puzzle. Place the first picture upside down and cover the entire back of the drawing or photograph with glue.

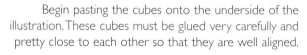

20

Begin pasting the cubes onto the underside of the illustration. These cubes must be glued very carefully and pretty close to each other so that they are well aligned.

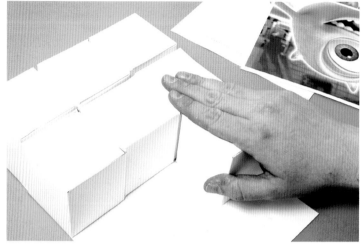

It is advisable to remove all lumps and pieces of glue from the back of the drawing or illustration because, if you do not do this, these imperfections will ruin the shape of the jigsaw puzzle.

21

With the measurements that you have noted down earlier in this exercise, you can create a 12-piece jigsaw puzzle that perfectly fits to the measurements of a standard A4 sheet of paper.

22

Without moving the jigsaw puzzle, and while the illustration dries, cover another illustration with glue and paste it on the top side of the twelve cube set so that you have an illustration on both sides.

23

Once the glue has thoroughly dried, identify the lines that separate the jigsaw puzzles´ inner cubes.

25

Repeat this process with all of the sides of the jigsaw puzzle, making sure that the pictures that are already glued are always facing in the same direction. By doing this, you will ensure that all of the cubes also *turn* in the same direction.

24

Use a ruler and a stanley knife to cut the dividing lines that separate the cubes of the jigsaw puzzle.

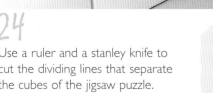

Do not forget to ask an adult to help you make the cut with the stanley knife.

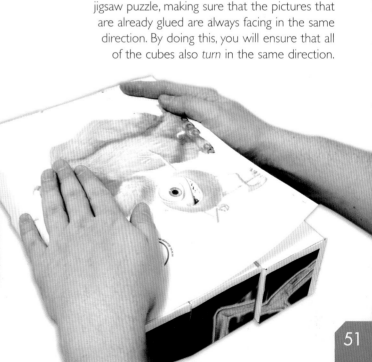

26
Once you have pasted on the six illustrations, let all of the cubes of the jigsaw puzzle dry thoroughly. The jigsaw puzzle will now be ready to play with!

8

Leaf and Dried Flower Press

Although paper and cardboard are fragile elements on their own, they can be made stronger when used in combination with other materials, as you will see in this leaf and dried flower press. The press is a wonderful device, as it will allow you to create magnificent floral prints for your natural science projects, or to decorate cards, bookmarks and invitations.

Tools and Materials

1. Thin cardboard: pink, light-green and dark-green
2. 4 X ¼" roofing belts and nuts measuring 60 mm in length
3. 4 X ¼" wing nuts
4. 8 X ¼" washers
5. Rubber stamp
6. White glue
7. Ruler
8. Two boards of wood
9. Pencil
10. Sandpaper
11. Thin cardboard
12. Cutting pad
13. Sheets of white silk paper
14. Carpenter's brace with 7 mm bit (or bigger)
15. Scissors
16. Stanley knife
17. Red acrylic paint

Leaf and Dried Flower Press

For this rather simple exercise, you will need to make holes in the wood. To do this, you will use a carpenter's brace, which is a tool that only an adult should use. So correctly mark the holes that must be made in the boards of wood and then ask an adult for help.

1

On each board of wood, mark a line parallel to each one of the sides at a distance of 2 cm from the edge. If you do it correctly, a frame should appear like the one shown in the picture.

2

At each one of the intersections of these lines, mark a small circle, which will be the reference point for the bolt holes.

3

Ask an adult to help you make the holes with the carpenter's brace. It is important for you to correctly mark the spots where the adult has to make the holes in both boards. Ask him or her to make the holes in both boards of wood at the same time. This way you will be sure that the holes in the top and bottom board match.

4

When making the holes, it is necessary for the carpenter's brace to pierce both boards completely, so that you have a wide hole in which to insert the bolts.

5

Since the wood has surely splintered a bit where the hole has been made, take a little piece of sand paper and sand the surface of the board. This will make the wood smooth again.

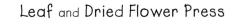

Leaf and Dried Flower Press

6

Trace the shape of one of the boards of wood onto a piece of thin cardboard. So that you can place more than one board in the press, the cardboard shouldn't be very thick.

7

Cut out the shape you have just marked on the cardboard. It is necessary for this shape to be correct, since this piece of cardboard will be the pattern for more pieces of cardboard. If you want, you can cut the cardboard with scissors, but if you get an adult to help you, it will be easier to cut it with a stanley knife.

8

Trace the shape of the cardboard onto another piece of cardboard and repeat this process of marking and cutting with at least seven pieces of cardboard altogether.

Leaf and Dried Flower Press

After you have cut out the seven pieces of cardboard, make sure that all of them have the same shape. If any of them need to be corrected, use scissors to cut them.

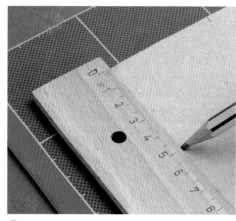

9

On one piece of cardboard make a mark at a distance of 5 cm from each one of the edges, that is to say, two marks on each side at a distance of 5 cm from each corner.

10

Join both marks so that you get a diagonal line forming a triangle in each corner.

11

Use scissors or ask an adult to help you use a stanley knife to cut the marks that you have just made, as shown in the picture.

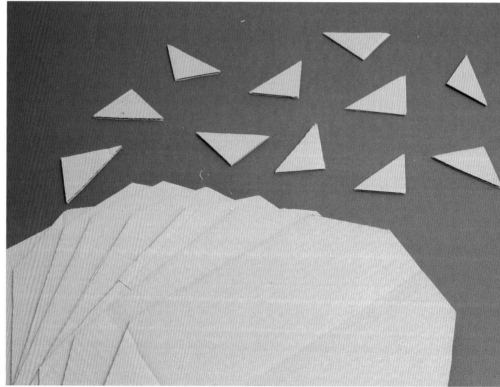

12

Trace this shape onto all of the pieces of cardboard and cut the corners off all of them.

13

Now prepare the paint to do the stampings. Place a little bit of red paint on a card and spread it slightly. Take the stamp and do some tests before stamping the flower shape on the pink card.

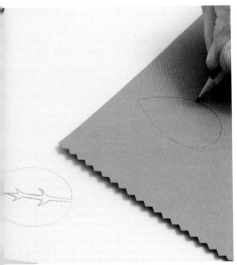

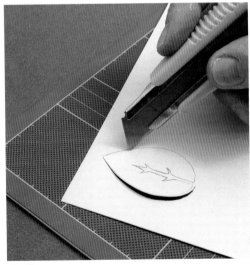

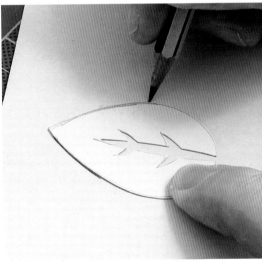

14

On the light-green and dark-green cards, draw the silhouette of a leaf. On the light green card, make a leaf with the inside cut out, as shown in the photograph. On the dark-green card, make a leaf without any interior relief.

15

With the help of an adult, cut the leaf shapes out of the card.

16

Trace the shape of the leaves on the dark-green and light-green cards.

Leaf and Dried Flower Press

17

Cut out the flowers that you have stamped on the pink cardboard. This way you will have a combination of flowers and leaves in three different tones.

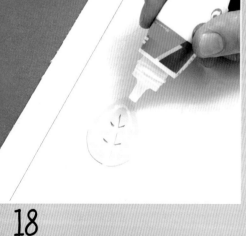

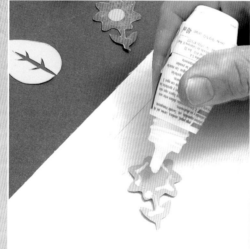

18

With white glue, carefully stick each one of the leaves onto one of the boards of wood. Create any design you like.

19

With glue, stick on the pink flowers that you have cut out and combine them with the leaves on the wood in order to make a design in the centre, or perhaps one that decorates the corners.

20

Carefully glue each one of the elements onto the wood and press down on them for a few seconds until the glue sticks to the wood, making sure not to deform the decoration.

21

As you can see in the picture, while you may only use a simple design, it expresses beautifully the function of the press.

22

In between each one of the pieces of cardboard, place a sheet of white silk paper folded in half. These sheets will help protect the cardboard from the moisture of the flowers and leaves that you want to dry and press.

23

Make sure that the pieces of silk paper all match neatly on one side. This way, they can be handled more easily and the press doesn't have to be taken apart each time you open it.

Leaf and Dried Flower Press

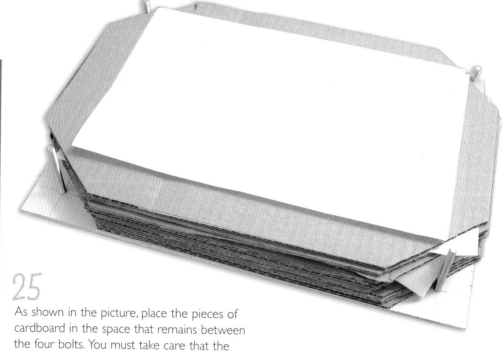

24

Insert a bolt in the board of wood that you have not decorated, making sure to insert all of the them in the same direction and using the holes you have pre-drilled. Use a washer for each bolt. This way you will protect the wood and prevent the hole from widening.

25

As shown in the picture, place the pieces of cardboard in the space that remains between the four bolts. You must take care that the pieces of cardboard are aligned correctly.

26

Now you can put the cover of the press in its place, inserting the bolts through the holes of the decorated wood.

If you want to press a flower or leaf, you have to carefully place them inside the silk paper in the press and tighten the bolts a little each day. This way you will get the flowers to dry and maintain their shape. If you adjust them too fast, you can ruin them.

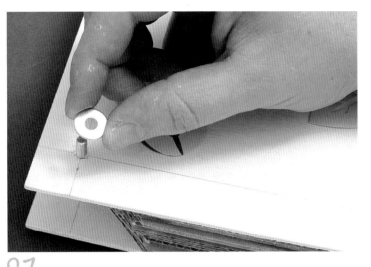

27

Place a washer on the top part of each one of the bolts, just as you have done with the bottom part of the bolt.

28

Now place the wing nut on the bolt and screw it on until it reaches the washer.

29

Adjust the pressure of the board of wood by tightening or loosening the wing nuts of the decorated wood cover. It is recommended that you tighten two of them at a time, adjusting the bolts that are in opposite corners to each other, as shown in the picture.

30

Now you can prepare any leaves, flowers or petals that you want to press and dry. Fold a sheet of silk paper in half and place whatever you are going to press in between the folded sheet.

Voilà!

Happy Crafting!